WRITING THE PICTURE BOOK

MASTERING THE FIRST BOOK ADULTS READ TO CHILDREN

WRITING LESSONS FROM THE FRONT, BOOK 10

ANGELA HUNT

Hunt Haven

ISBN: 978-1961394704, 978-1732412675
ebook: 978-1961394711

Sign up for Angela Hunt's newsletter for writers: angelahunt.substack.com.

WRITING LESSONS FROM THE FRONT

A Christian Writer's Possibly Useful Ruminations on a Life in Pages,
supplemental volume

INTRODUCTION

By 1987 or so, I had been a freelance writer for nearly five years. I wrote magazine articles mostly, when my small children were napping. I was content, because I became a writer in order to help my husband pay the mortgage. I had been told I had "a way with words," and I wanted a job I could do from home. Having worked very hard to bring children into our lives, I wanted to enjoy them while they were small.

So in 1983 I printed up business cards and declared myself a freelance writer. I began to read everything I could about the business of writing (which was not what I learned as a college English major), and soon I was writing magazine articles, catalog copy, almost anything people would pay me to write. I was a little amazed at how many people felt insecure about writing something as simple as a business letter. They hired me because I knew where the commas were supposed to go.

The more I wrote, the more I learned. And every time I got a new gig—for a new kind of writing—I would go to the library (this was pre-Internet) and get a book on how to write XYZ. I quickly discovered that being a writer is like being a builder. Once you learn how to use the tools properly—how to write a strong sentence, how to structure a paragraph, etc.—you can write anything from an essay to a novel, *as long as you follow the blueprint.* Every type of writing has its own blueprint, and setting out to write without knowing the blueprint is like a builder deciding to move from doghouses to Victorian mansions without knowing the first thing about Victorians or mansions.

One day I saw an ad in the back of *Writer's Digest* magazine. The ad was promoting a contest sponsored by Abingdon Press. They wanted to honor one of their writers, Lorna Balian, by finding a new picture book writer and publishing the newbie's book. Any unpublished picture book writer could enter if he or she sent in a manuscript and three sketches.

Well. I was an unpublished any-kind-of-book-writer, so I definitely qualified. I went to the library and got a book on how to write picture books, and studied the blueprint:

- Most picture books are 32 pages.
- Most picture books are less than 1,000 words.
- In a picture book, the pictures do half the work—
  they also tell the story, eliminating the need for
  many adjectives and descriptive phrases.

I'd been writing long enough to realize that "*most*" means "*industry standard.*" Deviating from the standard is risky because it almost always makes your book more difficult and expensive to publish.

So I sat down and wrote a story in about twenty minutes. Because I do not draw anything other than stick figures and horse heads, I found Diane Johnson, a local woman who had painted some beautiful murals at a nearby college. I visited her, explained the contest, and she agreed to do three sketches to submit with the manuscript. She put our package our package together (quite professionally!), and we sent it off before the deadline.

A couple of months went by, then I received a phone call from the children's editor at Abingdon Press. Mrs. Etta Wilson was happy to inform me that our book won first place and would be published. They would pay us an advance, too.

I was over the moon. We later learned that Abington had expected 100 entries, but over 455 came in from all over the U.S., Canada, and the Virgin Islands. Those were narrowed down to 25, then to 13, then to six. Etta told me that when there were only two entries remaining, the judges let a nine-year-old boy choose the winner. He chose our book, and *If I Had Long, Long Hair* became the winner.

Why did *Long Hair* win? I don't think Diane and I were any more talented than any of the other finalists, but we did follow the blueprint. I'm willing to bet that the 430 entries immediately eliminated did not.

If I had a nickel for every person who has come up to me and said they'd written a children's story, I could go live on a cruise ship and sail the world. Most folks say, "I made up this story for my grandkids, and they love it, so here it is—can you help me publish it?"

I know without reading a word that the story in front of me is not publishable. Why? Because the earnest man or woman offering it probably doesn't know there is a blueprint to follow.

People think that writing for children must be easy because children are simple, the books are short, and how hard could it be?

Honest answer? Very hard. Because a picture book has so few words, every word must be GOLD. Every word must pull its weight.

Picture books are costly to produce because color printing is expensive, so publishers do not buy picture books unless they are certain the book will sell. Mediocrity or merely *good* does not pass muster. So a picture book is one of the hardest types of books to sell.

You can always self-publish, but if you want your book to sell more than 100 copies, it had better be the best you can make it.

So that is why I've written this book. If you want to write a picture book, first you have to learn what you don't know . . . so you'll know what you need to learn. You have to understand the blueprint. You have to come up with a strong plot. And you have to know how to delight children.

Writing is both an art and a science, with both creative and mechanical aspects. You supply the creativity, and this book will supply the mechanics.

Like all of the **Writing Lessons from the Front** books, this book is brief. There are other books with philosophies and backgrounds and lots of full color illustrations on glossy pages, and this isn't one of them. This is a simple, practical book that will give you the nuts-and-bolts information you need to write a good picture book. Combine that with inspiration and your imagination, and you should be good to go.

Let's get started.

1

What Is a Picture Book?

LET'S begin by making sure we understand the definition of a picture book: it is a book designed to be read to a child, usually thirty-two pages long and less than 1,000 words, in which the art is an integral part of the story telling. Picture books are designed to be read in one sitting and they should delight children and the adults who read them.

A picture book is not an early reader, in which all words are chosen for their ability to be mastered by a beginning reader. Early readers often use words which come from word lists approved by education experts.

A picture book is not a story book, which is usually longer than 1,000 words and in which the illustrations, if any, supplement the storytelling. Most story books are designed to be read to a child, or by an older child alone, in small bits—a chapter a night, for instance. Charlotte's Web is both a children's novel and a story book.

I have seen many storybooks that aim to be picture books, but fail miserably on several counts: they are too long, too preachy, and clearly designed to appeal to well-intentioned adults rather than children.

When you write your first draft of what you hope will be a picture book, run it through this checklist:

- Is the manuscript less than 1,000 words? Fewer is better.
- Have you cut all **unnecessary** adjectives so the art can provide those details?
- Have you written it with page breaks in mind? Would the action in your story require more than 14 1/2 double page spreads? Do you have enough action to fill those page spreads? (More on this later).
- Would this story delight a child and the adult reader?

If your story does not meet those criteria, or if those things sounded like gobbledegook, keep reading.

*N*ot all picture books are the same, or even the same type. There are three broad categories, and genres within those categories. I once read a how-to book that gave the reader a personality quiz, then directed the would-be writer to a certain kind of picture book based on his or her responses. But you can write any type of picture book, as long as you know what the types are and follow the blueprint (sound familiar?) No need to limit yourself to one category.

The three broad categories are fiction, nonfiction, and concept books.

Fictional picture books are story books. They spin a fictional story to delight, entertain, and sometimes educate a child, in that order. No child wants to read an educational book that isn't fun, and no adult does, either. So if a story is intended to teach something, make sure the lesson is a by-product, not your primary intention. If you really want to teach, opt for nonfiction.

Nonfiction picture books aim to teach the reader about something—the history of pretzels, all about anacondas, or how farm animals live.

Conceptual picture books are often among a child's very first books. The classic *Pat the Bunny,* for instance, is neither fiction nor nonfiction, but teaches the concept of actions and textures. Many concept books encourage the child to interact with the book. A quick search on Amazon leads us to the following concept books: *Baby Touch and Feel Bunny, Never Touch a Porcupine!, See Touch Feel, My First Colors and Shapes,* and *Noisy Baby Animals,* complete with a button that plays recorded animal sounds. Other interactive books include flaps that lift up or fold out, to encourage the child to participate in the reading experience.

Many concept books are more expensive to produce because of their nonstandard formats and added features like buzzers, fabrics, and textures. Keep this fact in mind when you are considering the sort of book you want to write. Expensive books are harder to sell because a publisher takes a greater risk in producing them. If you have a concept book in mind, make sure it is unique.

PICTURE BOOK GENRES

This list is not exhaustive, because genres move in and out of favor every day. Some books may fit into more than one genre, but when you are starting out, make sure your book fits into at least one of the following:

1. Wordless books: the art carries all the work of telling the story.

2. Bedtime/nighttime/dreaming books: When do most people read picture books to their children? At bedtime. We shouldn't be surprised that bedtime books are a genre unto themselves, as they tend to quiet and calm children, preparing them for bed. These books often start off with a bang and then draw down to a satisfying ending. Example: *Goodnight Moon.*

3. Generational books: These books are about the link that

binds children to parents, parents to grandparents, and all family members. They demonstrate the circle of life and family love. These books may even appeal more to adults that to children. Example: *Calico Bear, Love You Forever.*

4. Adventure/monster/dinosaur books: What child doesn't love a monster? Combine a monster with adventure as in *Where the Wild Things Are*, and you have an amazing story any child will love.

5. Religious books: religious books can be overt or subtle, but will contain elements that reflect a particular faith. Many are retellings of Bible stories; others illustrate biblical or spiritual truths and values. Most explain religious lessons in simple ways a child can understand. But whatever your subject matter, make sure the book is delightful, not overly preachy or pedantic.

6. Counting books: Counting books teach children to count and illustrate the concept of numbers, including zero. Make certain, however, that the number of items pictured on a page matches the number being featured. If you're discussing the number 100, you'd better have 100 somethings in the illustration!

7. The folk/fairy tale: These books may be retelling of stories in the public domain, or new stories featuring fairy or folk tale conventions. They usually take place long ago in a nameless land far away, with larger than life characters that may have supernatural or magical powers.

8. Alphabet books: A is for alligator . . . B is for bumblebee. Alphabet books teach children the letters of the alphabet and usually feature spectacular art to complement the simple text. Many center around a theme, such as an alphabet book about animals.

9. Animal books: books about animals. I wouldn't put stories with animal protagonists in this category because animal protagonists are frequently employed when a writer

wants to approach an uncomfortable topic (An animal protagonist provides a certain amount of emotional distance). No
parent would read his child a book about a boy who is nearly
murdered for trespassing on his neighbor's property, but *The
Tale of Peter Rabbit* entertains us with a story about a bunny
who nearly ends up in a pie—like his father!— because he
didn't obey his mother.

Animal books teach children about farm animals, chickens,
dogs, cats, etc. They illustrate the animals, show the animals as
babies, and discuss what the animals do and where they live.
These are usually nonfiction, or story books that teach while
telling a good story.

10. Mash-up books: Combine two popular elements and
create a new idea: Example: *Dear Santasaurus*.

11. Poetry books: I am referring to poetry collections like
Mother Goose rhymes or stories that are music to the ear.
Rhyme can be used in a fiction or nonfiction book, but the
rhymes and meter had better be good, otherwise the result will
be weak. I'm always surprised to see how many beginning
writers work hard on their rhymes, but ignore the meter. It is
just as important, because the rhythm is important to a child.
Examples: Dr. Seuss books.

12. Books about ordinary life: These books deal with situations in a young child's life: getting dressed, going to the dentist
or doctor, getting a pet, the arrival of a new sibling, losing a
tooth. These may sound like humdrum topics, but the chal-
lenge is making these events fun, exciting, and fear-free! Example: almost any of the Mercer Mayer books.

13. The tale for all ages. Some books are enjoyed by adults
as much as or even more than children. *Love You Forever* is an
example, and *The Tale of Three Trees*. They are stories that
appeal to children on one level, and to adults on another. These
books have the potential to become classics, and sell year after
year.

. . .

THE NEXT TIME you go to the bookstore or library, sit down in the children's section, pull out some picture books, and read them. What genres do they belong to? Why do you think the publisher chose to publish those books? What makes them work? Learn to read picture books critically . . . when you're reading for yourself. When you're reading to a child, enjoy them!

*E*arlier I mentioned that before I begin to plot or write, I evaluate my idea. I do this for all my books, from adult novels to picture books, because this little acronym works wonders: WAGS. In order for your idea to work, your idea needs to have four elements.

W stands for *world*. Your story should take the reader to a world different from his own. In an adult novel, that means I would write a story that involves an unusual occupation, situation, or place. In my novels I've taken readers to the rain forest canopy, the world of the mortuary, medieval Ireland, and first century Jerusalem. The reader is interested in the story because he is visiting a world different from his own.

With children, the job is easier, because a child's world revolves around his room, his parents, and his home. Therefore virtually *everything* is a different world to him. The younger the child, the more true this is. For babies and toddlers, anything outside his home is a new world. For older children, anything outside the daily routine is new and different.

Fairy and folk tales carry readers to strange and distant lands. Daily life stories, in which a character goes to the dentist or doctor or library, explore those places and concepts. Animal stories illustrate the world of different animals—through fictional eyes. Rabbits don't wear jackets and sleep in beds like Peter Rabbit does. Bottom line: make sure there is something new in your story, a place or situation your child reader has not encountered before.

The A in WAGS stands for *active character.* Have you ever noticed that adults are usually absent or rarely seen in most children's stories? That's because the child protagonist must be the main character, not one of his parents. That why the adults in Charlie Brown cartoons sound like *Wonk wonk wonk,* because what they say doesn't influence the story. The story is perceived and driven by the children.

In other stories, the parents are away or dead or missing. Pippi Longstocking's parents are absent. *The Wizard of Oz's* Dorothy lives with her aunt and uncle, and she is separated from them at the point of the inciting incident. Alice falls through the rabbit hole and finds herself in a strange world without adult guidance. The children in the *Chronicles of Narnia* have been separated from their parents by war.

This absence of adults prevents the adults from doing what we parents usually do—taking over and taking power from the child. Children's books are all about giving power to the child, allowing him to make his own mistakes and learn his own lessons. So in your story, make sure the adults are offstage most of the time.

The G in WAGS stands for *goal.* Your protagonist should have a definite desire or goal that drives the action. She can state this goal up front, or she can state it after the inciting incident, when she has entered a different world. That's what happened to Dorothy when the tornado dropped her house in Oz. She stepped out, looked around, met some Munchkins, and proclaimed, "I want to go home." Then she spent the rest of the story working to fulfill her desire.

Finally, the S in WAGS stands for *stakes.* High stakes. Something should be at risk in your story. It may not be life or death, because we are dealing with children, but that's not far-fetched in a story for older children. If Dorothy doesn't meet her goal to go back to Kansas, she doesn't die, she simply lives apart from her loved ones for the rest of her life, and that would make her unhappy. What's at risk? Her happiness and the reunion with her loved ones.

In *A Gift for Grandpa*, the boy wants to give his grandpa a watch chain. If he doesn't succeed, he doesn't die, nor is he punished, but he fails to come up with the gift he wanted to give Grandpa. What's at stake? Grandpa's happiness and the boy's delight.

In *If I Had Long, Long Hair,* Loretta wants long hair that trails behind her, but eventually she realizes that having such long hair would be messy, inconvenient, and even invite rats and gerbils to make nests in her hair. So though her happiness —having long hair—is at stake, she abandons her desire because she realizes that she'll be happier if she remains just as she is.

Not every picture book will have these elements—for instance, *Good Night Moon* doesn't because it doesn't have a protagonist. It's not a story, it's a bedtime ritual designed to soothe children to sleep. Like *Pat the Bunny,* it's a concept book. But *Where the Wild Things Are* certainly does—Max wants to be a wild thing, so he's sent to bed without supper, where he dreams and travels to the island of the wild things where he leads the parade and is immensely popular, but he misses his family, so he wakes up (and abandons his desire) and finds himself in his own bed with his supper waiting for him.

WAGS. If your story idea meets these four tests, you are ready to begin plotting.

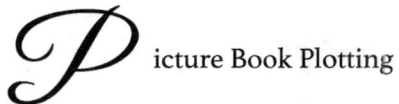 icture Book Plotting

YEARS ago I was asked to teach plotting to third graders. I came up with a "plot skeleton," and the concept was so simple, so visual, that now I teach it to adults and use it to plot my own stories. If you'd like to read a complete and thorough discussion, *The Plot Skeleton* is available as a booklet on Amazon.

Here's the visual:

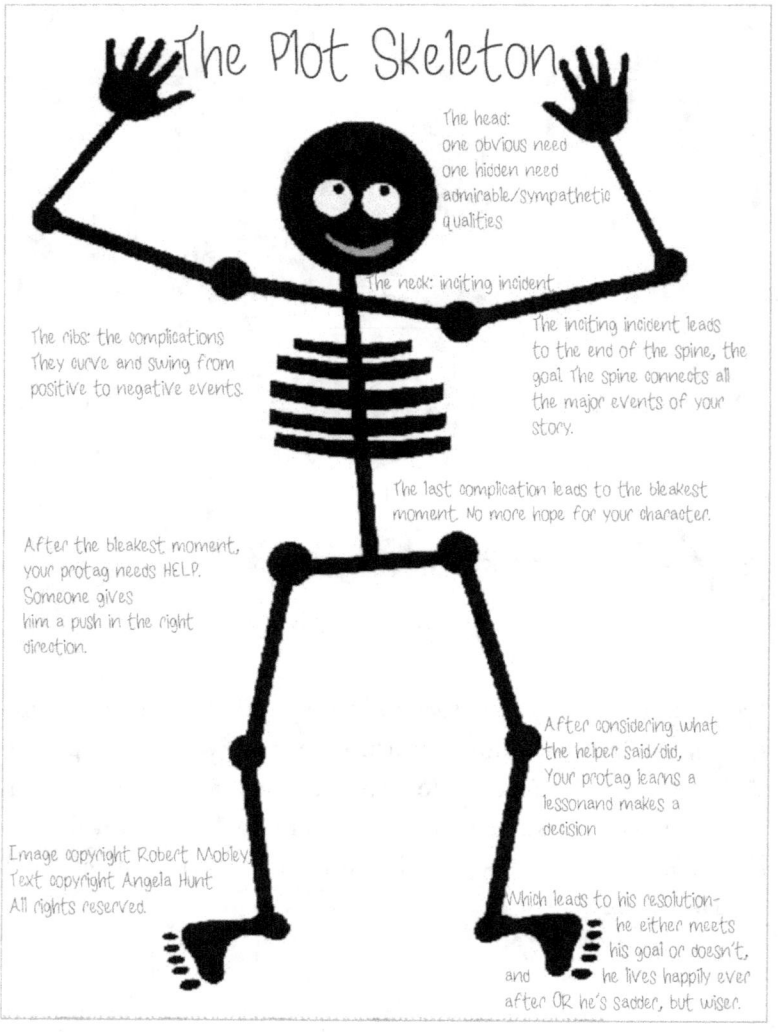

The Plot Skeleton

The head:
one obvious need
one hidden need
admirable/sympathetic
qualities

The neck: inciting incident

The ribs: the complications
They curve and swing from
positive to negative events.

The inciting incident leads
to the end of the spine, the
goal. The spine connects all
the major events of your
story.

The last complication leads to the bleakest
moment. No more hope for your character.

After the bleakest moment,
your protag needs HELP.
Someone gives
him a push in the right
direction.

After considering what
the helper said/did,
Your protag learns a
lesson and makes a
decision

Which leads to his resolution—
he either meets
his goal or doesn't,
and   he lives happily ever
after OR he's sadder, but wiser.

USING the plot skeleton is simple: we come up with story bits for the "bones" of the story, beginning with the skull. Note: since picture books are so short, all of the story "bones" are usually present, but may be hard to spot—and sometimes they don't appear in the order listed below. But for a story—any story—to work well, it should be supported by a solid plot skeleton.

The **skull** represents the main character, the protagonist. A lot of beginning writers have a hard time deciding who the main character is, so settle that question right away. Even in an ensemble cast, one character should be more predominant than the others. Your child reader wants to place himself into your story world, and it's helpful if you can give him a sympathetic character with whom he or she can relate. Ask yourself, "Whose story is this?" That is your protagonist.

At the very beginning of your story, this main character should be dealing with two situations, which I represent in the skeleton by two yawning eye sockets: one obvious desire, one hidden need.

Usually the first few chapters of a novel are involved with the business of establishing the protagonist's world, his needs, and his personality. In a picture book, you rely on the art to set the story time and world because you only have a few pages to introduce the reader to your main character. So keep it brief, but put all the elements in place.

Your story kicks into gear when you move from the skull to the spine, a connection known as the *inciting incident*.

In a picture book, the inciting incident is often signaled by two words: "One day . . ." Those two words are a natural way to move from setting the stage to the action. As you plot your story, ask yourself, "One day, what happens to move my main character into the action of the story?" Your answer will be your inciting incident, the key that turns your story engine.

Your character stated or showed us his driving desire in the first few pages. After the inciting incident, your character sets out to achieve his goal.

In my book *The Singing Shepherd*, we learn that Jareb is a shepherd who lacks courage. His unspoken desire (shown, not told) is to be brave. Then one night something happens . . . an invitation is issued, but Jareb is too afraid to accept it.

The inciting incident in *Peter McPossum's Wiggles and Giggles* occurs on page one. His parents receive an invitation, but Peter is too wiggly, so the opening pages are all about him learning to control his wiggles and giggles.

. . .

IN *TOO MANY TUTUS,* Lola Li loves tutus. The inciting incident occurs when she receives a box from her Nana—and it's filled with tutus! So she makes a plan to enjoy them all.

"I hope you like these," her note said. "You can wear a different one every day of the week."

One day my nana sent me a big surprise box.

IN *THE CHICKEN Who Loved Books,* Little Red loves it when Henry brings books to the coop and reads them to the chickens. But (inciting incident), one day Henry doesn't bring a book, so Little Red makes a plan to turn that situation around. Her desire is to get books back to the coop!

One day Henry didn't bring a book to the coop.   He brought a little flat toy instead.

WHAT WOULD HAPPEN if your protagonist achieved their desire right away? That would result in a boring book! So you need complications that prevent the protagonist from getting what he wants, represented by the curving ribs in your plot skeleton. A novel might have 100 complications, but a picture book only needs three.

Why three? Because even in the shortest of stories three complications works better than two or four. I don't know why three gives us such a feeling of completion, but it does.

The complications are a good place to inject humor and surprise.

In *IF I HAD LONG, Long Hair,* Loretta dreams of having long hair
. . . until she realizes it could cause serious problems.

IN *A GIFT FOR GRANDPA*, the boy wants to buy his grandpa a watch chain . . . But even though Grandma promises that God is faithful, they seem a long way from getting the watch chain.

YOUR THIRD COMPLICATION should be the worst complication you could think of (that would be suitable for children)—something the protagonist cannot solve on his own. It will lead your main character to his or her bleakest moment.

At the bleakest moment, your character needs *help*, but be careful how you deliver it. The ancient Greek playwrights had actors representing the Greek gods literally descend from a structure above in order to untangle their complicated plots and set things to rights. This sort of resolution is frowned upon in modern literature. Called *deus ex machina* (literally *god from the machine*), this device employs an unexpected and improbable incident to bring victory or success. If you find yourself whipping up a coincidence or a miracle after the bleakest moment, chances are you've employed deus ex machina. Back up and try again, please.

Avoid using deus ex machina by sending a helper, represented on the plot skeleton by the thigh bone. Your character obviously needs help; if he could solve the problem alone, he would have done it long before the bleakest moment.

So send in the cavalry, but remember that *they can't solve the protagonist's problem*. They can give him a push in the right direction, they can nudge, they can remind, they can inspire. But they shouldn't wave a magic wand and make everything all right. Whatever you do, do not send in an adult to solve the problem. Children are on a continual journey to become less and less dependent on their parents, so having an adult solve the problem is antithetical to their growth process. Let your protagonist solve the problem himself.

In *A Gift for Grandpa*, the boy and his grandma needed a new horse, but since they only had a dollar, they wanted to buy a watch chain. Through a series of events and Grandma's willingness to help others, they end up with a horse . . . but no watch chain. In my original draft, I had Grandma run out and cut off a portion of the horses's tail to braid a watch chain, but my editor wisely and correctly told me the *boy* should be the one who supplies the gift. Indeed he should! I changed the text, and learned a lesson from the experience—children's stories are about empowering children, and helping them learn to solve their own problems. Incidentally, the same principle holds true in all stories. In *The Wizard of Oz*, the good witch doesn't send Dorothy back to Kansas; Dorothy sends herself to Kansas once she realizes that there's no place like home.

You may be hard pressed to cite the lesson you learned from the last novel you read, but your protagonist needs to learn something. This lesson is the *epiphany*, a sudden insight that speaks volumes to your character and brings them to the conclusion of their inner journey.

James Joyce popularized the word *epiphany*, literally *the manifestation of a divine being*. (Churches celebrate the festival of Epiphany on January sixth to commemorate the meeting of the

Magi and the Christ child.) After receiving help from an outside source, your character should see something—a person, a situation, or an object—in a new light.

When the scarecrow asks why Glenda waited so long to explain the power of the ruby slippers, the good witch says, "Because she wouldn't have believed me. She had to learn it for herself."

The scarecrow then asks, "What'd you learn, Dorothy?"

Without hesitation, Dorothy announces that she's learned a lesson: "The next time I go looking for my heart's desire, I won't look any farther than my own back yard."

What does your protagonist learn in the course of his trial? What has he realized about his life, his past, or his future? Does he appreciate something or someone he used to take for granted? Write down what your character has learned, then show us how he can put this knowledge into action. Armed with this new realization or understanding, what does your protagonist do that he could not do before?

THE BOY in *A Gift for Grandpa* learns that God supplies our needs and even our wants in unexpected ways.

The birthday horse waited outside for Grandpa as we took the silky horsehair into the house. Grandma helped me braid it into the most beautiful watch chain we had ever seen.

Then we wrapped Grandpa's gift and waited for him to come home.

In *THE TRUE PRINCESS*, after spending a long time living as a commoner, the princess learns that it's not jewels and satins that mark a daughter of the king, but love.

YOUR STORY SHOULD END with a changed protagonist—he or she has gone through a profound experience and has changed as a result, hopefully for the better. When he reenters his ordinary world, he has a new understanding to share with others.

How will you visually illustrate your character's change?

PLOT DISSECTION: **Brandon takes a Bath**

To illustrate how simple plotting by skeleton is, let me present the script to one of my picture books. It should be easy to see how it all comes together in even a simple little story like this one.

I've put my comments in brackets.

[The opening: the protagonist's (Brandon's) ordinary world:
]

. . .

P. 5: Yesterday I spent the day at my cousins' house. Aunt Molly, Uncle George, and my cousins Sam and Tricia are calm, quiet people, but Brandon is something else.

P. 6-7: Brandon played outside in the mud and wrote on himself with colored markers. At dinner, he put spaghetti on his head. It was a messy, dirty day. [Obvious need: a bath. Hidden need: like all little kids, Brandon needs to know he's loved.]

P. 8-9: After supper Aunt Molly asked, "Brandon, are you ready to take a bath?" [The inciting incident: Mom's invitation.]

Brandon shook his head. "No," he said. "I'm not ready to take a bath." [Brandon's goal: avoid the bath! Bathtime signals an end to the day, an end to his fun.]

[We move into the Story World: the bathroom.]

p. 10-11: "But Brandon," Uncle George said, "if you take a bath you will be clean and sweet-smelling." [He's urging Brandon toward the tub.]

Brandon made fish faces at Tricia. "I'm not ready to take a bath." [Brandon counters by doing something else. This pattern will be repeated many times.]

P. 12-13: "BRANDON," Aunt Molly said, "I'm giving the bath water a squirt of bubbling super soap. You can soak in mountains of bubbles."

Brandon twirled on his toes and said, "I'm not ready to take a bath."

P. 14-15: "BRANDON," Sam said, "I'm putting my toy boat in the tub. You can sail it."

Brandon stood on his head and said, "I'm not ready to take a bath."

P. 16-17: "BRANDON," Tricia said, "I'm putting toy dishes in the tub. You can pretend to pour milk and coffee."

Brandon somersaulted across the floor. "I'm not ready to take a bath."

P. 18-19: "BRANDON," Aunt Molly called, "I'm putting your beach bucket and shovel in the tub. You can scoop up bubbles and put them in the bucket."

Brandon marched like a soldier and said, "I'm-not-rea-dy-to-take-a-bath."

P. 20-21: "BRANDON," called Uncle George, "I'm blowing up your swimming ring seahorse for the tub."

Brandon started pulling the laces out of his dad's sneakers. "I'm not ready to take a bath."

P. 22-23: "BRANDON," Sam said, "I'm putting Howard in the water. You can swim with your pet turtle."

Brandon found the day-old lollipop he'd stuck under the table. "I'm not ready to take a bath."

P. 24-25: "BRANDON," I said, holding up a bottle from the kitchen, "I'm squirting green drops in your bath water. You can play in colored bubbles!"

Brandon hopped like a rabbit and squeaked. "I'm not ready to take a bath."

. . .

P. 26-27: Uncle George sighed and turned to Aunt Molly. "I suppose we could skip bathtime and move straight to bedtime. Because Brandon simply doesn't want to take a bath." [The opposition closes in, leading to Brandon's bleakest moment—though, because it's a children's story, it's only bleak to a child.]

"Now I do," Brandon shouted. "But there's no room for me in the tub!" [Cornered, Brandon takes the most favorable option.]

P. 28-29: "No PROBLEM," said Uncle George. "We'll make room."
Uncle George took out the seahorse.
Aunt Molly took out the bucket and shovel.
Sam took out the turtle and the boat.
Tricia took out the toy dishes.
But I couldn't take the green drops out of the water. [The unseen narrator acts as helper. She has inadvertently provided Brandon with a means of escape.]

P. 30-31: Brandon took off his dirty clothes and climbed in the tub. He splashed and played, and played and splashed. Finally he called, "I'm ready to get out!"

"OH NO!" Aunt Molly said, peeking at him. "He's green!"

"Brandon," said Uncle George, "Wouldn't you like to take a nice, clean bath?"

P. 32: Brandon shook his green hair and climbed out of the tub. "Not now. I'm not ready to take a bath!" [Resolution:

Brandon runs out of the bathroom, heading back to his ordinary world of play and fun with two easy-going parents and siblings.]

SEE how the bones of the story come together? Sometimes you may not find it necessary to represent every "bone" of the story, because many times that element can be implied. But once you get a sense for how the bones fit together, you are well on your way to constructing any kind of story you please.

NOW YOU'RE ready to begin writing. Put your major story elements on note cards, if you like, and number a blank sheet of paper from one to 32. These are the pages in your picture book.

Pages 1 and 32 are half-page spreads.

Page 2 is usually dedicated to the copyright notice.

Page 3 may have a dedication.

Page 4 may be blank, or it may be combined with page 5 to open the book with a double page spread.

From this point on, put brackets around each even and odd number: 6 and 7, 8 and 9, etc. Those are your double page spreads. You may use them as one unit, or you may use each page as a separate unit, depending on how much action is in your text. The child reader expects to see each major action playing out.

If you write, for instance.

Zeke rode his bike until he met Tom. Then he and Tom went to the fair.

The reader will expect to see a bike, Tom, and a fair. You could do riding the bike and meeting Tom on one page, and going to the fair on another, or you could do them together on a double page spread. Just be certain that the text goes on the page where the action is illustrated.

Consider your story, and assign each element and/or major action to a set of bracketed pages: for instance, "Brandon dancing away from daddy, page 8-9."

Do this for all 32 pages, and when you have finished, you will have laid out your picture book plot. You've conquered the biggest hurdle. Now work to polish your prose and make certain the story works.

Whenever I find myself bogged down in a story or something seems out of place, it's invariably because I've gone down a rabbit trail or become unfocused. Whenever that happens, I pull out my plot skeleton and remind myself of what it is my characters are working toward. What is their hidden need, and how are they changing so it will be met? What is their desire or goal, and how do their current activities either push them toward their goal or pull them away from it?

With a little reminder from my scrawny plot skeleton, I am back on my way within minutes.

Now it's your turn. Go plot something wonderful.

elight

IN THE INTRODUCTION, I told you that a picture book should delight children . . . and the adult reading the story. How do you do that?

Humor delights. What do children find funny? Funny words and sounds, funny situations, and the unexpected.

Rhythm delights. Many picture books delight children because they have a repeating refrain the child can repeat as the story progresses. Like "I'm not ready to take a bath" or "If I had long, long hair, I'd . . ."

As an adult I was absolutely delighted by Joyce Maxner's *Nicholas Cricket*, a book that can turn any reader into a musician. The book is poetic and rhythmic, and you can't help but fall into the cadence of the words and rhythm. The story is simple—at night, the bugs come out to play in the Bug a Wug Band, and the other bugs dance—but the magic of the story is in the rhythm of the words. Try saying "Moonlight glows and summer wind blows" as "peep-peep-peepers come dancing through the vines" and "rabbits come dancing on tip-tippy toes" because

"the music is just so grand.

The music is just so grand.

The music is just so grand."[1]

Art delights. Whether you or the publisher chooses the art, make sure it fits the tone and text of your story. One of my stories, *The Singing Shepherd,* was first published in 1992, and the art was rather formal and still. I had previously released *The Tale of Three Trees,* and I think the publisher wanted to "brand" the second book in a similar style and format.

But *Shepherd* is not the same kind of story as *Trees*. It features humor and exaggeration, so after the book went out of print, I republished the book and hired my own artist. The second edition is much more suited to the story of *The Singing Shepherd.*

Angela Elwell Hunt

THE SINGING SHEPHERD

Illustrations by Peter Palagonia

By the author of the best selling
The Tale of Three Trees

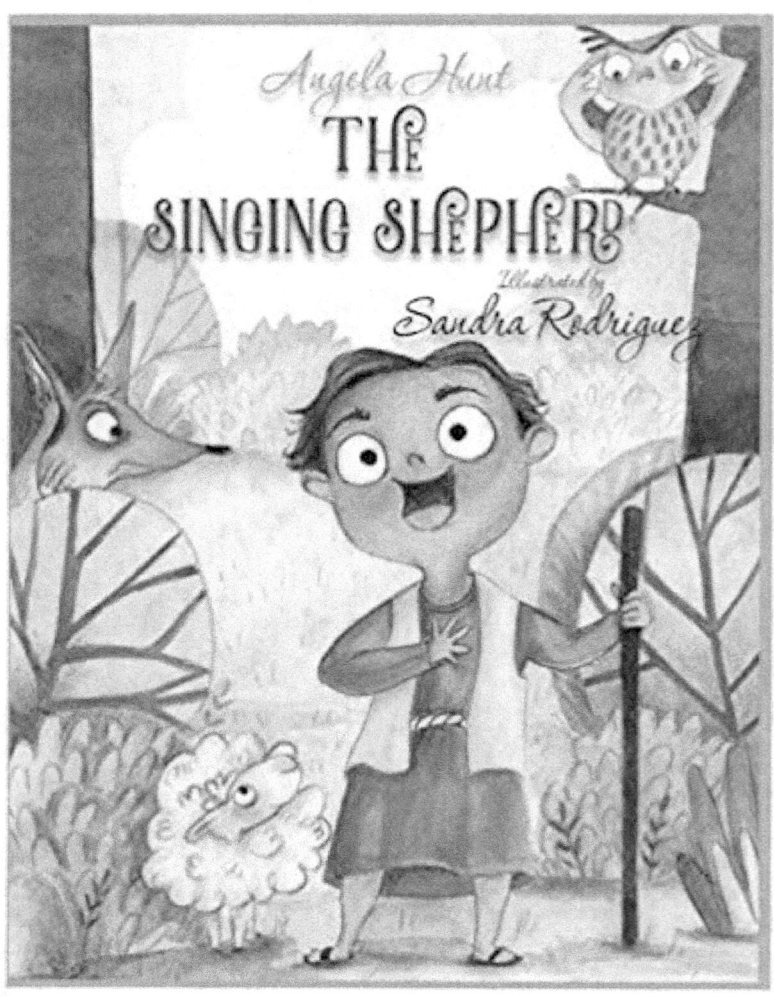

How can you tell if a book will delight children? Find some children and read it to them. Go to your public library and read it to some children at story telling hour (ask the librarian for permission first). Read it to children at your church. Read it to your grandchildren. But don't take the grands' word for it—they're biased.

Notice where the children laugh (or don't laugh), and where they fidget. Not every child will react the same way, of course, but look for the overall responses. Do a blind test—mix your story in with other books, and see how they react to yours compared to how they react to others. When you read the other stories, notice what the author does to elicit responses from the children. How can you incorporate that technique into your work? (Don't steal the author's words or ideas, but notice and use his or her techniques).

The best way to remember how children think is to spend time with them. It's good for the soul. And the best way to learn how to write a picture book is to read lots of them. They're good for the soul, too.

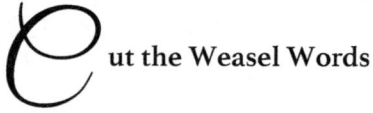

6

Cut the Weasel Words

So you've written a story and it's two thousand words. Too long. How can you shorten it without losing the gist of the story?

First, take your manuscript and a yellow highlighter. Read through the story and highlight any adjectives. Ask yourself, "Can the art supply these details?" If it can, cut the unnecessary words. But sometimes you want adjectives for artistic or rhythmic purposes, and that's okay. My book *If I had Long, Long Hair* just wouldn't be the same if I cut the adjectives and it became "If I Had Hair."

Second, you may have too many complications in your plot. Did you fit everything into the page spreads on your numbered page? If you have more story than you have page spreads, you probably need to cut some actions or complications. Keep it simple.

PERHAPS YOU HAVE TOO many characters. If two characters are serving the same purpose, delete one. If your protagonist Sam has two best friends, give him one.

MAKE sure you don't have a paragraph of preaching at the end of the story. Children are more intuitive than we realize. You don't have to explain the moral or point of the story; the child will figure it out.

ASIDE: I wrote a book called *The True Princess*. It's a Christian parable disguised as a fairy tale, about a beautiful princess who wears fancy clothes and lives in a palace. One day her father has to go away, but he leaves her with Nana, who teaches her how to live like a normal village girl. When the princess is lonely, Nana comforts her until her father the king returns.

One day I read the story to a group of kindergarten children at a Christian school. I asked them who the king represented, and they knew: God! Then I asked who Nana represented. The teachers were surprised when a little boy raised his hand and said, "The Holy Spirit!"

He was right. Children are clever, and you don't need to spell things out. Let them learn the lesson for themselves.

PERHAPS YOU'VE WRITTEN TOO much in the first act. You don't have to give us the protagonist's life story or any backstory at all. Just start the story and move forward. A sentence or two of introduction is usually enough. The art will show us who he/she is, where they live, and what era the character lives in.

NOW LET's tackle the weasel words. What's a weasel word? It's a word that clutters up your manuscript. Some of them are common to almost everyone who speaks English; others are unique to each writer. For instance, after I handed in one book, the editor called and said I was using *pull* too much.

I was flabbergasted. "Pull?"

"Yes," she said. "You have people *pulling* into driveways, *pulling* onto roads, *pulling* things from their purses and pockets. The word is all over the place."

I shook my head. "I didn't realize."

But I went back and did a search for the word *pull* in my manuscript—and there it was, sprinkled like paprika every few paragraphs. I deleted some, changed some to *turned*, others to *took*, others to *tugged*. But now I'm much more aware of my use of the word *pull*.

TOOLS FOR TRACKING

The best tool for tracking down your weasel words is your word processing program's search and replace feature. If you write in any of the standard programs—Word, Word Perfect, Scrivener, Pages—you will find *search* (or *find*) and *replace*. When you're searching for a particular weasel word, ask your program to search for the word with spaces before and after it (unless it's a word likely to be used several times at the end of a sentence. In that case, you'll want to omit the last space).

For instance, if I was searching for *it*, I would enter [space]it[space] in the search box. Then I'd enter [space]IT[space] in the *replace* box. If you forget to add the spaces, the program will capitalize every instance of *it* in your book, and you'll have to manually change them back to what they should be.

That's what I do for every weasel word on my list. I use search and replace to find the word or phrase (with spaces), then I replace it with the exact same word or phrase, except in all capital letters (also with spaces before and after). This doesn't change any of my prose, but those weasel words now LOOM on the page and catch my attention as I work through subsequent drafts. And every time I see one, I stop and ask myself if I can make the sentence better without that word. If I can, great. If I can't—or if it would make the sentence too convoluted—the sentence remains as it was.

IDENTIFYING the Weasel Words

The first weasel word is one I first noticed the year I taught high school English. I'd never thought of it as a weasel word, but suddenly there it was, all over my students' papers. I grew weary of circling it with my bright red pen, and over and over again I drew little weasel faces in the margins of their papers.

A very small, very overused word. Can you guess what it is?

Yes! IT!

It is so common we really don't think about it, but sometimes we fall into patterns that result in what I call "vague its." This particular species of *it* has infested many a sentence. When you find one of these, the best thing to do is shoot it and start over by asking, "What am I really trying to say here?"

Example: Mary wore a blue dress with flowers on *it.*

Does that *it* cause you to stop or slow down in any way? Can you tell immediately what *it* represents?

Yes, the blue dress. You shouldn't have to think too long about that *it,* so it's a good *it.* You could keep it, though you cut even more words by writing:

Mary wore a blue flowered dress.

The *it* that weakens your prose is found in sentences like this:

It is hard to get a drivers' license.

Hmm. What does that first *it* stand for? You have to think a moment, don't you? *It* has no apparent connection to anything else in the sentence, the paragraph, or the world.

So back up and say what you're really trying to say:

Getting a driver's license is hard. Or complicated. Or whatever you really meant.

What about this example:

"You don't understand," Mom said, sniffling. "*It's* so hard to live without your Dad."

In the second example, the questionable *it* is found in dialogue, and we loosen up when considering dialogue because people talk in all kinds of ways. If your character doesn't use proper grammar when she's crying and upset, she's just like the rest of us. Welcome her to the human race, and let her keep her undefined *it*.

Pardoning Reasonable Weasels

Please understand that the principles I'm presenting here are not hard and fast rules. I'm not saying every *it* should be condemned. Writing is part craft and part art, and I would never want to infringe on anyone's art . . . as long as they knew what they were doing. But when people make a word mess and call it art, well . . . I'm not likely to read it.

Doesn't mean everyone will feel the same way.

So if you want to write *It's the way he smiled that made me love him*, no one's going to demand that you be tarred and feathered by the writer police.

But as you sit down to revise and edit your manuscript, it's a good idea to search for *[space]it[space]* and replace it with the same term, but in capital letters. Look at each of the *its* you find in your manuscript, and see if each one is clearly related to the word it represents. If so, fine, no problem. But if you have a disturbing number of the noisome vague *its*, perhaps you should consider their eradication.

PASSIVE VERBS

We are a video generation. We have grown up with film and television and instant-everything. We microwave and keep the Internet at our fingertips. We Google for information, we call up maps in our cars, and we can even send emails through our refrigerators.

So why wouldn't you want words that move at the speed of life?

You're probably familiar with the *to be* verbs: *is are am was* and *were*. These are passive words, and sometimes they have their place. Sometimes you want to say "The sky was a blue dome overhead" and be done with it.

But at other times we pull out the passive verbs when other perfectly active and visual words are within arm's reach.

If I write *the cat was on the table*, what do you see the cat doing as the sentence plays out in your mind? You're not really sure, are you, because the verb *was* is a wimpy little verb that doesn't pull much weight. If you do a search/replace and replace every *was* with *WAS*, you'll be able to go through your manuscript and replace every wimpy *was* with a hunky anything else.

You could write:

The cat yawned on the table

The cat reclined on the table

The cat retched on the table

The cat curled itself on the table

The cat lay on the table

The cat died on the table

The cat stretched on the table

... the possibilities are endless.

I always search for *was* and *were* in every draft and replace them with capitals because I want to see if I can find something better. Sometimes I stick with the simple *was*. Most of the time I find a better, more active way to write my sentence.

If I'm writing in present tense, of course, I search for *am* and *is* as well. I won't replace every active verb, but at least I *consider* its replacement. That consideration is what teaches us to write tighter.

Weak Adjectives and Enabling Adverbs

An adverb, by definition, is employed to support a verb that isn't doing its job. So be brave and search for ly[space], replace it with LY[space], and you should corral a small herd of shifty adverbs. For each of them, either see if you can replace the weak verb with something stronger, or simply cut the adverb. You'll do your manuscript a big favor.

Someone once reminded me that Jesus taught people by using nouns and strong verbs . . . and we all know how long people have been repeating *His* stories.

Cut the Obvious

My high school English teacher told us we should pay ourselves a quarter for every word we can cut. Cutting makes a manuscript stronger.

True story: on at least two occasions I have taken novels that had gone out of print and sold them to another publisher. But before I handed in the old manuscript to a new publisher, I asked if I could edit it again. Why? "Because," I told one of my editors, "I write tighter now, and I want to improve it."

On those two occasions, I took the manuscript and without

deleting a single line of the plot, I cut over nine thousand words from the book. How? By cutting out statements of the obvious like She stood ~~from her chair.~~ Three words, three quarters.

He clapped ~~his hands.~~ (What else is he going to clap, unless he's a walrus?)

They ~~all~~ stood ~~to their feet.~~ (Ditto. Unless they stand on something else, lose the unnecessary words.)

She nodded ~~her head in agreement.~~ (A nod means agreement.)

He stood ~~up.~~ She crouched ~~down.~~ (You can almost always get rid of *up* and *down.*)

She scratched her head ~~with her hand.~~ (Unless she's using her ballpoint pen to take care of the itch.)

She ~~reached out and~~ accepted the trophy.

Do you see how quickly those unnecessary words can add up? So spare a few trees and develop a sense for spotting extraneous verbiage. Then cut, cut, cut.

The Thing about That

I overuse *that* all the time. It slips into my language, my thoughts, and my writing. So whenever I start to cull the weasel words, I do a search for *that*, replace it with THAT, and then carefully consider every THAT I come across. I don't know a test for it except to read the sentence without it—if the sentence makes sense without the THAT, I take it out. If the sentence seems to be missing something important, I leave the *that*. Simple.

Miscellaneous Weasel Words

Other weasels on almost every list of overused words are *just, very, rather, began to, started to, some,* "*of the*," "*there was,*" and *suddenly.*

Just is used too much. You may want to leave it in dialogue, because people do use it in casual conversation, but in nonfiction writing or narrative, you'll probably want to omit *just*. Or replace it with *simply* where applicable.

Very often comes off as amateurish unless it's in a character's dialogue. Remember—the more concise the writing, the stronger the writing, so your sentence will probably be stronger without words like *very*.

Why write *he began to run* or *he started to eat,* when you could write *he ran* or *he ate?* Unless you purposely want someone to be in the process of beginning an activity, the simple past tense will do. But if you want to write:

As he began to eat, a shot rang out, shattering his pasta bowl,

Then *began to* is best.

"Of the" is often used in formal titles (The Sword of the Lord and of Gideon), but if you find yourself writing *he hid inside the cloak of the knight,* then ditch the *of the* and write *he hid in the knight's cloak.* Much, much cleaner.

"There was" is a passive verb linked to a nothing word. So if you find those constructions in your book and you didn't write it for a purposeful reason, cut the nothing words and figure out what you're trying to say. Instead of

There was a peaceful haze over the valley . . .

write

A peaceful haze hovered over the valley.

SUDDENLY: In fiction, if you are writing and a shot rings out, to your characters it has rung out *suddenly* whether you use the word or not. See for yourself:

She bent to breathe in the scent of the sweet flowers. "Thank you for the lovely bouquet," she told the little girl. She pressed a kiss to the child's forehead and slipped her fingers around the beribboned stems, ready to hand the flowers to her waiting attendant—

A shot rang out.

She turned, saw horror on her attendant's face, and felt a dull pressure in her back, but that had to be the result of walking all day, from bending to receive dozens of little bouquets, from kissing children and shaking hands and smiling until her jaws ached like they ached now, but no, the pain was lower, but it wasn't pain exactly, it was pressure, and then she heard a splatting sound and felt something splash her shoes, probably the children, maybe a child had spilled a bottle of water, but as she looked down she saw that the water was red, as red as her dress, as red as the single rose the prince had left on her pillow this morning—

SORRY—I got a little carried away with my sinister fairy tale that is clearly NOT a picture book.

Do you see how you don't need *suddenly* to write a sudden action? If it occurs unexpectedly, it will *feel* sudden.

Unless a character's house is on fire or he's running for his life, you will probably want to lose the **exclamation points.** Too many comes across as amateurish—as though you're working too hard to convey an emotion or sense of urgency. So reserve them for truly dire circumstances, if you use them at all.

Find more elegant ways to convey emotion or urgency through dialogue, interior monologue, or action. And remember—sometimes an emotion is stronger if it's understated.

Quiet can be intense.

. . .

THOSE SUGGESTIONS ARE a few ways to help you whittle down your word count. Remember who will be reading this story: a tired adult, home after a busy day, putting the children to bed. The adults don't want to read a long story.

Think of the artist—he or she has to fit a lot into a page spread or two, plus leave room for the text. Too much text means too little space for the art.

And think of the child—he's tired, he's ready to sleep, and he wants to hear a story, not a word salad. So choose the words that count, and lose the rest. Your story will be the better for it.

he Art

A PICTURE BOOK is half text, half art. The artist does a lot of hard work, and if you negotiate a shared royalty deal, they deserve half the royalties.

Remember when I told you that my first picture book won a contest and was published as a result? I mentioned that Diane Johnson did three sketches to send in with the manuscript, and on the basis of my text and her art, we won. First prize was publication and an advance, which we split 50/50.

But at that point, my work as a writer was done, and Diane had to do the hard work of illustrating the entire book, including cover and title page. She worked a day job as a graphic artist, so she had to do the work in her free time on evenings and weekends. She would work hard on a sketch, paint it, and send it in . . . and many times she had to make adjustments to suit the editorial board. (This was before we could send things with a click of a computer key!)

Diane did a beautiful job on the book, but when I sold my second picture book to Abingdon Press, they asked Diane if she wanted to illustrate it and she said no. Working a full time job and illustrating books on a deadline was just too much (and I don't blame her for turning the job down).

Never think art is easy—it's every bit as demanding as coming up with a good idea and writing a story.

So once you have your picture book text ready to go, how do you find an artist?

If you are seeking to be traditionally published, where a publisher buys your manuscript, gives you a contract, and pays you an advance, you don't have to worry. That publisher should have an art/design department, and they will design your book and find an artist to do the illustrations. Lots of beginning picture book writers think they need to submit art with the text, but don't do it! They could not like the art and reject your book, so that practice cuts your chance of acceptance by 50 percent. The only occasion to submit both text and art to a traditional publisher is if YOU are a professional artist and you are submitting an entire package. Some people have the talent to do both. I don't.

If, however, you want to self-publish your book, you need to find your own artist. Trust me—do not ask a friend. You may think your friend is a great artist, but most artists have a distinctive style, and you ought to compare several artists' styles to see which one best suits your book.

For years I have used the talented artists at 99designs.com to illustrate my self-published picture books. Artists from around the world have samples of their work on 99design s.com, and you can look through the different illustrators' work and find the ones you like. Then you can invite those artists to participate in a contest or work one-on-one with you to illustrate your book.

I held contests for several of my books, creating a brief

stating exactly what was required: illustrations for an 8x10 picture book that would be published and available on Amazon. It would require 13 double page spreads and two single page spreads, as well as a cover and title page. I would supply the manuscript, and I wanted to have the work done by (date). I always added this: *I would like to have the work submitted by the deadline, but I would rather have good than fast, so please consider that date flexible.*

I understand that life happens. The last artist I worked with was working on her way to meeting the deadline, but then her daughter was struck by a car, which put her behind schedule. Of course I understood. I would rather have a mother care for her daughter than go crazy trying to meet my deadline.

Not every illustrator on 99Designs has done picture books, so I always remind them of several things:

- the illustration needs to conform to the text. Don't draw five pigs if the text says there are four.
- Keep text and important visual elements away from the page edges and the gutter (the space in the center of a double page spread). These areas may be cut off during the printing process.
- Place the text on a separate layer so the font can be changed or the text edited without harming the art.
- I always ask the artist to send me the files in Photoshop format. Some people may prefer InDesign, but I don't have that program and Photoshop lets me do everything I need to do.

You'll need to set a budget for your project and let the artists know what that is. I'm hesitant to put a number here because such things change, but I can tell you this: let it be at *least* $1,000. That is a lot of work. Artists who accept deals on 99designs and other such sites sign a release when the work is done, giving all the rights to the owner/author. Technically, it is a work for hire, and you will be the owner of the illustrations when all is done. This will be a relief for you when you are publishing your book—you won't have to keep track of dividing royalties and paying the artist her share every year.

I know that some professional graphic artists frown on sites like 99designs and say that those artists don't earn a living wage. Not an American living wage, perhaps, but I did some research and learned that the amount I paid an artist in Indonesia was enough to feed his family for a month. And don't all writers start out writing for pennies a word? I did. As a newbie, I was grateful for an opportunity to write and enlarge my portfolio. So I believe in programs like 99designs, and have used artists from Indonesia, Britain, Germany, Slovakia, and the U.S. All of them were super-talented and I have been delighted with the results.

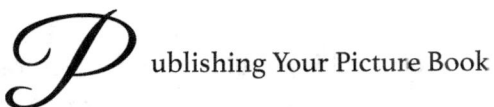 ublishing Your Picture Book

WHICH IS BETTER, traditional or self-publishing?

Without a doubt, traditional publishing is best. If you sell your book to a traditional publisher, they will handle the publishing, the artwork, the design, the editing, the sales, and the distribution. That last one is HUGE. They will see that your book is placed into brick-and-mortar bookstores, and that is where people pick up picture books, read them, and buy them for their children and grandchildren.

Beware of subsidy or vanity publishing. These folks ask YOU to pay while they edit, sell, and distribute your book. But their distribution consists mainly of listing your book on Amazon.com and other online sites, so no one is hand-selling your book. Most bookstores will not purchase books from subsidy publishers, so you book will be one title in a sea of other self-published books. Unless you are hand-selling your book, reading your book in schools, and spending your own money to promote it, it will sell maybe one hundred copies.

Did I say I have self-published several picture books? Yes —but I do the editing and designing myself. I took a few basic classes in graphic design and I learned how to use Photoshop, so I can take the digital files I receive from the artist and adjust the text, size a cover to certain specs, and upload the files to sites like Amazon.com and BarnesandNoble.com. Several of my self-published picture books were originally traditionally published, so I hired artists to do new illustrations (because the old illustrations were owned by the publisher) OR I asked the original artists if they'd give me permission to use their art and I send them a royalty check every year.

So why don't I try to traditionally publish my new picture books, if traditional publishing is so much better? Several reasons:

- Time. It takes months to sell a picture book, and about a year to bring it to publication. I'd rather not wait because I have already developed a readership, though most of my books—and readers—are for adult novels. Picture books are a lovely distraction for me.
- The market. When publishing hits upon hard times, children's books are often the first to be eliminated. As I mentioned before, they are expensive to produce, and the market is smaller.
- Selling. Not many agents represent children's books (for the above reasons), and I don't want to deal with selling it myself.
- Control. I'm not a control freak, but it *is* nice to be able to arrange, write, and publish a book on my own terms.

- Money? Actually, money is not a primary consideration. A traditional publisher would probably give me an advance, and that's always nice, but the royalty would be only about 6 or 7 percent because the other half of the typical royalty goes to the artist. Still, a traditional publisher should sell more copies than I could as a self-publisher.
- Self-publishing can bring a royalty ranging from 35-70 percent, but you need to remember that a color book is going to be more expensive to print than a paperback novel. The retail price is going to be higher (thus handicapping sales), so your total royalty is going to be lower.

How Do You Self-Publish a Picture Book?

The process isn't complicated, but it can be a little tricky when you're first getting used to it. I like to keep things simple.

Picture books today are primarily sold in three formats: ebook, hardcover, and paperback. I would recommend ebook and hardcover. Color paperbacks can be nearly as expensive to print as hardcovers, and as a parent, I would want all my kids' books to be tough because kids can be hard on books! I still have the picture books I bought for my kids, and now my grandkids read them.

To publish a hardcover version of your book, I recommend the program at IngramSpark.com. You can publish an ebook (ePub format) and a print version by entering the basic information and uploading a cover and a pdf file containing the entire book.

If you are not skilled with Photoshop, you might want to hire a graphic artist to create PDFs of your individual book spreads, then combine all of them into one file.

Ingram Spark will provide a cover template, so you or your graphic artist will need to fit your cover onto the template and upload it in CMYK format and high resolution. Ingram Spark has details on their website.

Note: CMYK format (refers to the color mode of an image) is for printing on paper. Your pages for the print edition should all be saved in CMYK format.

RGYB format works best for the jpeg files you'll use for your ebooks. This format looks best on digital screens.

Your ebook will be in a fixed layout format—the text won't be resizable on an ebook reader. To create a book for Kindle, download the free **Kindle Kids' Book Creator** and load your book pages into the program. It's easy to use—just drag and drop the pages in the correct order, enter the appropriate information, and click. Within seconds you will have a mobi file, which you can upload to the Kindle Publishing Program as your Kindle ebook. Amazon KDP also will allow you to turn that ebook into a paperback if you want, but that's up to you. Amazon KDP does not offer hardcovers at this time.

I have not covered every detail—you'll need to learn about ISBNs, pricing, etc. —but you can find that information online at whichever publishing outlet you choose. An ISBN is the international book number—every edition of a book has its own number. Amazon Kindle will give you a free ISBN for your Kindle book, and you can purchase one at Ingram Spark.

Why Write a Picture Book?

If there's not a lot of money to be made, and if the work is exacting, then why write picture books at all? For love.

I love kids, I love the way they think, and I love explaining the world to little ones through story. I love writing those stories, and using humor to illustrate deep truths. Picture books are an art form I enjoy, so that's why I do it.

(And to be completely honest, after paying an artist, it takes a *long time* for me to actually make a profit on self-published picture books.)

If you don't love reading picture books, you should probably write something else. You can write chapter books for older kids, middle grade books for ages 10-14, or young adult books for teenagers. You can write anything . . . as long as you study the blueprint and know how to use the tools.

But if you love children, and writing, and art, picture books might be your perfect niche. You may have such a gift that you can easily sell to traditional publishers, so please follow your heart. If you are serious about pursuing the art of picture books, you should join the Society for Children's Book Writers and Illustrators, the largest organization of children's writers and illustrators in the world. You can find more information about them at their website: https://www.scbwi.org.

I wish you every success on your journey of creating art and wonder for children.

EXERCISES

1. Find some children ages 3-8. Ask them about their favorite stories. What sort of things do they like to hear about? Monsters? Aliens? Transformers? Make a list.

2. Using the list you've just made, come up with three different story ideas with WAGS. Stories that will take the hearer to a different world, with an active character who has a definite goal that involves high stakes.

3. Write out your three stories—don't worry about editing, just write out the stories and let the words flow.

4. Find some more children in your target age group. Tell them your stories and see how they respond. If they are less than delighted, ask them how the stories could be improved . . . and then make those changes. Chose the best of the three stories to polish and consider for publication . . . but only if you're getting really strong feedback from children (who are not related to you).

PICTURE BOOKS BY ANGELA HUNT

The Tale of Three Trees

The Singing Shepherd

Nat the Brat

Calico Bear

The True Princess

Peter McPossum's Wiggles and Giggles

Too Many Tutus

The Sleeping Rose

The Chicken Who Loved Books

A Gift for Grandpa

Pretzels by the Dozen

Bathtime for Brandon

If I Had Long, Long Hair

Howie Hugemouth

NOTES

Chapter 5

1. Joyce Maxner, *Nicholas Cricket*. New York: Harper Collins, 1989.

ABOUT THE AUTHOR

Angela Hunt writes for readers who have learned to expect the unexpected from this versatile writer. With over five million copies of her books sold worldwide, she is the best-selling author of more than 160 works ranging from picture books (*The Tale of Three Trees*) to novels and nonfiction.

Now that her two children have grown, Angie and her husband live in Florida with Very Big Dogs (a direct result of watching *Turner and Hooch* too many times). This affinity for mastiffs has not been without its rewards—one of their dogs was featured on *Live with Regis and Kelly* as the second-largest canine in America. Their dog received this dubious honor after an all-expenses-paid trip to Manhattan for the dog and the Hunts, complete with VIP air travel and a stretch limo in which they toured New York City. Afterward, the dog gave out pawtographs at the airport.

Angela admits to being fascinated by animals, medicine, unexplained phenomena, and "just about everything." Books, she says, have always shaped her life— in the fifth grade she learned how to flirt from reading *Gone with the Wind*.

Her books have won the coveted Christy Award, several Angel Awards from Excellence in Media, and the Gold and Silver Medallions from *Foreword Magazine*'s Book of the Year Award. In 2007, her novel *The Note* was featured as a Christmas movie on the Hallmark channel. She has completed a doctorate in biblical literature and her doctorate in Theology.

When she's not home writing, Angie often travels to teach writing workshops at schools and writers' conferences. And to talk about her dogs, of course. Readers may visit her web site at www.angelahuntbooks.com.

www.ingramcontent.com/pod-product-compliance
Lightning Source LLC
Chambersburg PA
CBHW061317120626
46546CB00007B/2628